Rescuing Whales

by Marianne Lenihan

Scott Foresman
is an imprint of

Glenview, Illinois • Boston, Massachusetts • Chandler, Arizona
Upper Saddle River, New Jersey

Photographs

Every effort has been made to secure permission and provide appropriate credit for photographic material. The publisher deeply regrets any omission and pledges to correct errors called to its attention in subsequent editions.

Unless otherwise acknowledged, all photographs are the property of Pearson Education, Inc.

Photo locators denoted as follows: Top (T), Center (C), Bottom (B), Left (L), Right (R), Background (Bkgd)

Cover Getty Images; **1** Craig Bailey/Florida Today; **3** DK Images; **4** Craig Bailey/Florida Today; **6** Littleny/Shutterstock; **9** DK Images; **12** Getty Images.

ISBN 13: 978-0-328-51392-5
ISBN 10:   0-328-51392-X

9 10 VOFL 16 15 14 13

Whales are sea mammals. Many people like whales for the melodies of their songs. Whale songs have been called symphonies.

Usually, whales swim the seas easily. But sometimes they get stuck in shallow water or grounded on a beach. This is known as being stranded or beached.

When a whale is stranded, its body weight presses on its heart and lungs. The whale can have a hard time breathing. Also, the whale's body temperature can become very high without the cooling seawater. Its skin can dry out, crack, and become sore.

Here's how people help stranded whales: The whales are surrounded by volunteers and scientists. They pour cold water and chipped ice on the whales to keep them cool. The scientists use their supplies to do medical tests on the whales.

Sometimes all that stranded whales need is to be kept cool and calm until the tide rises. Then the rescuers herd the whales into a group and push them out into deeper water. If the whales find a deep channel of water, they are able to swim out to the open sea.

Scientists do not fully understand why whales strand. One idea is that the lead whale becomes sick and swims off course. Then the other whales in the pod follow. Another thought is that harsh weather, such as blizzards and hurricanes, may upset the whales' sense of direction.

In 1986, at Eastham, Massachusetts, three young pilot whales stranded. They had come into a shallow bay.

Scientists were called to help. A crowd waited anxiously on the beach until they arrived. The scientists checked the whales. They decided to take them to an aquarium for care.

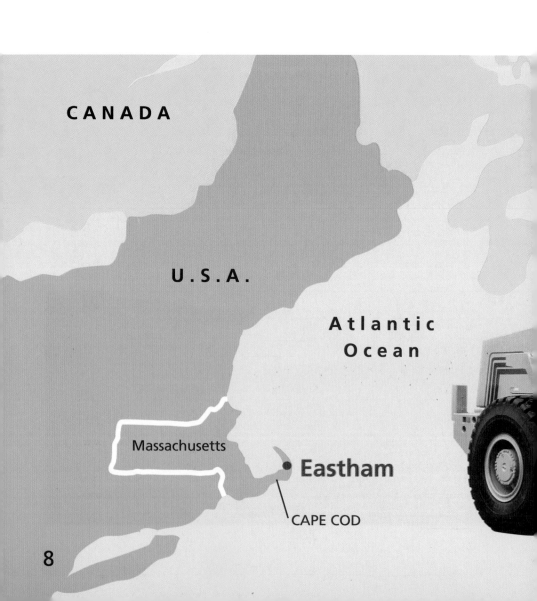

CANADA

U.S.A.

Atlantic Ocean

Massachusetts

Eastham

CAPE COD

The young whales were placed on stretchers. Then, front-end loaders lifted each whale into a truck. Only the front-end loaders could move the heavy whales. One by one, the three whales were lifted and placed gently into the truck.

At the aquarium a crane moved the whales out of the truck and into a tank. It took the young whales a few days to get used to aquarium life. They were fed small fish stuffed with vitamins and medicines.

This journal shows what happened on the day the whales were ready to be returned to sea!

WHALE RESCUE JOURNAL

8:00 A.M. Most of the water is drained from the aquarium tank.

9:00 A.M. The whales are lifted out of the tank on stretchers.

10:00 A.M. The stretchers are lifted by cranes into a truck.

11:00 A.M. The truck drives the whales to a large ship.

2:00 P.M. The whales are loaded onto the ship.

4:00 P.M. The ship sets sail for deep ocean waters.

6:00 P.M. The scientists on the ship search for a pod of whales.

7:00 P.M. A pod of whales is spotted. Scientists fit each whale with a special radio tag to help track the whale.

8:30 P.M. The stretchers are lifted by a crane. The whales are lowered into a special cage next to the ship.

12:00 A.M. The whales have gotten used to the ocean water again. The cage is opened. The whales swim out to meet their new pod. Everyone cheers!

Whales know when they're in trouble. Usually, they cooperate with their human rescuers. Although some whale rescues are not successful, many whales have been returned safely to their ocean home!